9/15

NATURE'S CHILDREN

BLACK WIDOW SPIDERS

by Katie Marsico

Children's Press®

An Imprint of Scholastic Inc.
New York Toronto London Auckland Sydney
Mexico City New Delhi Hong Kong

Content Consultant
Dr. Stephen S. Ditchkoff
Professor of Wildlife Sciences
Auburn University
Auburn, Alabama

Photographs © 2014: age fotostock/NHPA: 36; Bob Italiano:
44 map, 45 map; Dreamstime: 5 top inset, 11 (Gordon Miller),
2 background, 3 background, 44 background, 45
background (Matt Antonino); Getty Images: 24, 25
(J. Robinson), 15 (Kimberly Hosey), 8, 9 (Michael
Leach), 20, 21 (Robert Llewellyn), cover (Steve
Maslowski); Minden Pictures/Premaphotos: 6,
7; National Geographic Stock/Mattias Klum:
39; Newscom/Bernard Weil: 5 bottom inset,
40; Science Source: 32, 33 (Francois Gohier),
28 (James H. Robinson), 4, 5 background, 30, 31
(Nature's Images), 12, 13 (Scott Camazine); Shutterstock,
Inc.: 1, 22, 23 (Jose Gil), 35 (Matteo photos); Superstock,
Inc.: 19 (Cusp), 2 spider, 26, 27, 46 bottom (FLPA); Thinkstock/
iStockphoto: 16, 17.

Library of Congress Cataloging-in-Publication Data
Marsico, Katie, 1980–
  Black widow spiders / by Katie Marsico.
  pages. cm. — (Nature's children)
  Includes bibliographical references and index.
  Audience: Ages 9–12.
  Audience: Grades 4–6.
  ISBN 978-0-531–21225-7 (lib. bdg.) —
  ISBN 978-0-531–25435-6 (pbk.)
  1. Black widow spider—Juvenile literature. I. Title.
  QL458.42.T54M373 2014
  595.4'4—dc23   2013019582

Printed in China 62
SCHOLASTIC, CHILDREN'S PRESS, and associated logos are
trademarks and/or registered trademarks of Scholastic Inc.

1 2 3 4 5 6 7 8 9 10 R 23 22 21 20 19 18 17 16 15 14

Black Widow Spiders

Class	Arachnida
Order	Araneae
Family	Theridiidae
Genus	*Latrodectus*
Species	*Latrodectus hesperus, Latrodectus mactans, Latrodectus tredecimguttatus, Latrodectus variolus*
World distribution	Areas with temperate climates; every continent except Antarctica
Habitat	Warm, dark, quiet environments such as rock and wood piles, garages, sheds, basements, crawl spaces, and rodent burrows
Distinctive physical characteristics	Average length up to 1.5 inches (3.8 centimeters) including legs; average weight less than 1 ounce (28.3 grams); body diameter 0.25 inches (6.4 millimeters) for adult females, with males generally smaller; two main body segments; females have a reddish hourglass marking on underside of abdomen; exoskeleton is shed during periods of growth; four pairs of eyes; sensory hairs covering legs
Habits	Build silk webs; trap prey in webs and wrap prey in silk; use fangs to deliver toxic bite; lay eggs; do not care for young after hatching; mainly live solitary lives; females occasionally kill and eat males after mating
Diet	Feed mainly on ants, flies, cockroaches, mosquitoes, grasshoppers, beetles, and caterpillars

Contents

CHAPTER 1

Waiting in the Web

At first, the cottony web seems completely still in the morning sunlight. But it shakes every few seconds as a fly struggles to escape. The fly's efforts are useless. Suddenly, a different animal causes the web to stir.

A black widow spider waiting nearby closes in on its prey. It uses its hind legs and spinnerets to wrap the fly in a tightly wound case of silk. The spider then pierces the trapped insect with its venom-filled fangs. Soon the web is still once again as the black widow feeds on the motionless fly.

Black widow spiders are famous for their powerful bite. Their fangs pack venom 15 times stronger than that of a rattlesnake. But black widows are far more than just ferocious killers. They are amazing arachnids that scientists are eager to learn more about.

Insects such as grasshoppers are no match for a black widow's deadly web.

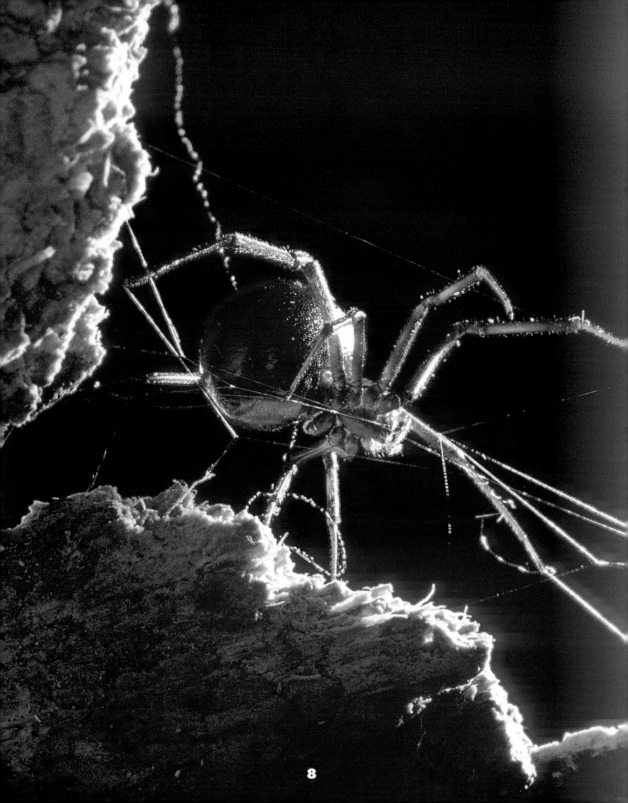

Drawn to Dark, Quiet Areas

Black widow spiders are the most venomous spiders in North America. They are also found in temperate regions all over the globe. This includes parts of every continent except Antarctica.

Black widows prefer to live in warm, dark places. They often spin their webs in piles of wood or rocks. As a result, people sometimes accidentally bring black widow spiders into their homes when they carry firewood inside. Black widows also nest in garages and sheds. They are found in basements and crawl spaces. In addition, they sometimes live in burrows dug by rodents and other small animals.

A black widow spider's web features irregular crisscross patterns and tangles of silk. The main part of the web is usually shaped like a funnel. The web's thick silk frequently feels sticky and coarse to the touch.

FUN FACT! Though male black widow spiders are smaller than females when it comes to overall body size, they tend to have longer legs.

Black widows are rarely seen out in the open sunlight.

Physical Features

Female black widows measure up to 1.5 inches (3.8 centimeters) long, including their legs. They are typically 0.25 inches (6.4 millimeters) in diameter. They weigh less than 1 ounce (28.3 grams). Males tend to be smaller than females.

Like all spiders, black widows have eight legs that are covered in tiny hairs. Their body is split into two main segments. The first segment is called the cephalothorax. It contains the spider's eyes, fangs, and pedipalps. It also holds the stomach, brain, and special glands that produce venom. The second segment is called the abdomen. This is where the spinnerets are located.

Black widows can have different color patterns depending on their location. In North America, female black widows are shiny and black. They have a red, hourglass-shaped marking on their abdomen. Males generally have lighter coloring. They have a brown stripe down the middle of their back, as well as white or yellow streaks.

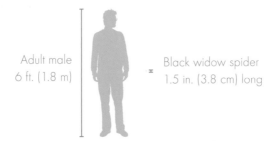

Adult male
6 ft. (1.8 m)

Black widow spider
1.5 in. (3.8 cm) long

A female black widow's markings help set it apart from similar-looking spiders.

CHAPTER 2

Incredible Arachnids

Black widow spiders have many remarkable features that have helped them succeed as deadly predators. These arachnids are famous for their venomous bite. Both male and female black widows have glands near their fangs that produce powerful venom. A black widow's venom works by attacking its victim's nervous system. This causes intense pain and makes it difficult for prey to breathe and move.

Adult female black widows have larger venom glands than males or younger spiders do. This makes them more dangerous to humans. Luckily, black widows do not usually attack humans unless they are trying to defend themselves. They prefer to hunt prey such as ants, flies, and cockroaches. They also prey on mosquitoes, grasshoppers, beetles, and caterpillars. These spiders face few threats except for humans. The only wild animals that prey on black widows are certain types of other spiders, various species of wasps and birds, alligator lizards, and praying mantises.

Sticky web threads keep prey from escaping as a black widow approaches and prepares to feed.

Fangs and Feeding Habits

Black widows do not rely on big teeth to deliver their deadly bite. Poison travels from their venom glands to a pair of small, hollow fangs. Like most spiders, black widows do not truly eat their victims. Their bite injects a special enzyme into their prey. This enzyme breaks down the prey's body into a liquid form. The spider then sucks the juicy meal into its stomach.

Spiders tend to have a slow metabolism. This means they do not need to eat every day to survive. Black widows also do not need to go out on the hunt. They can lie in wait for their prey to wander into the dangerous tangles of their webs.

FUN FACT! Some black widows can go up to 90 days at a time without eating.

A black widow's fangs are located on the tips of its jaws.

14

15

Superior Silk

Black widows can produce extremely strong silk. The sticky threads used in black widow webs are made of the strongest spider silk in the world. The webbing can also stretch easily without splitting. Some experts are trying to learn more about how this incredible silk works. Their research might help people create everything from high-tech sports gear to lightweight body armor!

Black widow spiders mainly use their strong silk to build webs that trap prey. Webbing also helps defend against possible predators. Wasps or other enemies that come too close often get tangled before they are able to attack the spider. Once an animal becomes caught in the web, a black widow uses the stiff hair on its hind legs to wrap more silk around its prey. This makes it harder for the victim to fight back when the spider approaches to inject its venom.

FUN FACT! The tips of a black widow's legs are oily. This prevents them from getting trapped in the sticky threads they spin.

A black widow uses its legs to pull silk from its body and spin it into a web.

A Spider's Senses

Black widows have four pairs of eyes. However, their vision is very poor. Scientists believe that these spiders can tell the difference between light and dark. Yet it is unlikely that black widows rely on eyesight to spot prey.

In addition, spiders do not have ears. This means they do not listen for sounds the same way human beings do. Instead, they sense sounds using tiny hairs that are mainly found on their eight legs and pedipalps. These hairs are extremely sensitive to vibrations. This enables black widows to detect even the slightest movement within their web.

Spiders also rely on special sensory hairs on their legs and pedipalps to detect tastes and scents. Instead of licking with a tongue or sniffing with a pair of nostrils, they use these sensory hairs to collect chemical information about various flavors and smells.

A black widow's eyes are located near the top of its head.

Spider eyes

Spider eyes

A Different Kind of Skeleton

Like other arachnids, black widows do not have bones on the inside of their body. They instead have a stiff exoskeleton. The exoskeleton provides support and protection from the outside. This tough outer covering also helps prevent arachnids from losing moisture and body fluids.

Movable joints connect the different pieces of the exoskeleton. Spiders have muscles inside their exoskeleton that allow them to bend their legs inward. They depend on blood flow to create pressure that helps them extend their legs outward.

Like all spiders, black widows must molt to grow larger. Arachnids molt by moving their muscles back and forth to loosen the old exoskeleton. Their heart rate also speeds up. This causes blood to flow from the abdomen to the front half of their body. This forces apart a black widow's old outer covering. A new exoskeleton is revealed underneath.

A spider uses its eight spindly legs to move quickly across a variety of surfaces.

Warning Signs

Scientists believe that the color patterns found on many female black widows are important to the spiders' survival. Since these spiders hang upside down in their web, predators such as birds are able to see their underside as they fly above. The red hourglass marking of a female North American black widow acts as a warning sign to these enemies. Experts have noticed that when certain predators spot the pattern, they tend to look for food somewhere else.

The few animals that do hunt black widows do not necessarily die after eating these venom-filled arachnids. However, the spiders' enemies sometimes experience stomach problems after feeding on them. This is especially common when a predator eats a female black widow. This is because females produce more venom than males do.

A female black widow's red marking is one of its most recognizable features.

A Black Widow's Life

Black widow spiders typically live for one to three years in the wild. They are usually solitary animals. This means they prefer to spend their time alone instead of in groups. In fact, black widows often attack and kill other spiders that venture into their webs.

The only time black widows spend time together occurs in spring and early summer. This is when black widows come together to mate. Before mating, a male slowly and carefully enters a female's web. It is important that males move cautiously so that females do not think an enemy is approaching.

A male black widow taps the female's web with his leg as he approaches. This tapping is like a code that sends a message to the female. It tells her that a mate is nearby.

A small, weak black widow male is more likely to be eaten by a female than a strong one is.

Mate or Meal?

Black widows are famous for their violent mating habits. It is not uncommon for the female spider to eat the male after mating is complete. However, this does not happen every time black widows mate. Other types of spiders also demonstrate the same behavior after mating.

Scientists believe that females feed on their mates simply because they are the nearest available meal. A female black widow must take in all the nutrients she can as she prepares to lay hundreds of eggs.

During mating, a female spider stores the male's reproductive cells in her body. This means that female black widows do not need to mate more than once each year. A female that has mated even a single time is usually able to produce several groups of eggs.

Male black widows have larger pedipalps than females.

From Egg Sac to Spiderlings

Before laying eggs, a black widow spins a round or pear-shaped bundle of silk in her web. This cocoon is called an egg sac. It will house the spider's unborn babies. Most female black widows produce between 5 and 15 egg sacs during their lifetime. Each sac contains roughly 200 to 900 eggs.

A female black widow stays close to her eggs after laying them. She carefully guards the egg sac against possible predators. It takes about 10 to 30 days for the spiderlings to hatch.

Females do not care for their young after they leave the egg sac. This means that the spiderlings are on their own from the moment they hatch. The young spiders face several immediate dangers, including the threat of being eaten by other babies in the web. It is not uncommon for hungry black widow spiderlings to attack and devour one another.

Each black widow egg is about 0.5 to 0.6 inches (12 to 15 mm) in diameter.

Approaching Adulthood

Black widow spiderlings leave their mother's web within a few days of exiting the egg sac. They use a process known as ballooning to travel out of the web. During ballooning, baby black widows release silk threads into the air. These threads catch the wind and blow the baby spiders to a new area. They eventually land in different locations. The spiderlings build their own webs and learn how to trap prey.

Young black widows are called nymphs. They reach adulthood within two to four months of hatching. They molt several times during this period. They also change color. At first, most North American black widows are various shades of white, yellow, and orange. As they molt, they develop the color patterns of adults.

Young black widows are not dangerous to human beings. But females' venom glands eventually become larger and more developed. By the time they are adults, they are ready to use their fangs to deliver their potentially deadly bite!

Only a few spiderlings from each black widow egg sac survive to adulthood.

CHAPTER 4

Past and Present

Black widows belong to the genus *Latrodectus*. This genus is made up of approximately 31 spider species worldwide. All of them are venomous. Experts estimate that five species of *Latrodectus* are found in the United States.

Scientists first identified the genus in 1805. However, spiders have existed on Earth since long before then. Fossils show that the earliest spiders lived between 416 and 359 million years ago. This means that they were present hundreds of millions of years before the last dinosaurs walked the planet.

Scientists are still working to figure out how the toxins that flow through a female black widow's fangs became so powerful. This involves learning more about the various species of *Latrodectus* that live in the United States and beyond.

This ancient spider's body has been preserved in amber for about 45 million years.

A Sampling of Species

Three of the most common species of black widow spiders found in the United States include the northern black widow, the southern black widow, and the western black widow. The northern black widow spider mainly lives in the northeastern part of the country. It is also found in portions of southeastern Canada. Southern black widows exist in the southeastern United States. They have been seen as far west as Texas and Arizona. Western black widows spin their webs throughout western North America and various parts of Mexico. The females of each of these three species display the red hourglass markings that many people think of when they picture black widows.

Other members of the genus *Latrodectus* look slightly different. Mediterranean black widows live in Europe and Asia. They do not have an hourglass pattern on their underside. Instead, they have red or orange spots on their upper side.

A Mediterranean black widow's markings look much different than those of a North American black widow.

A Few Facts About False Widows

False widow spiders belong to the genus *Steatoda*. They are part of the same family as black widows. However, there are a few major differences between the two genera. For example, false widows usually pose less of a danger to humans than true black widows.

People sometimes mistake members of *Steatoda* for various *Latrodectus* species, though a closer look shows that they are not identical. A false widow typically has an oval-shaped abdomen. The abdomen of a black widow is more rounded. In addition, false widows do not have the same red color pattern on their underside as most female black widows do.

Scientists have identified about 120 species of *Steatoda* worldwide. These spiders frequently feed on prey such as cockroaches and wood lice. Certain false black widows kill and eat true black widows as well!

The noble false widow is the most venomous spider in Great Britain.

CHAPTER 5

Learning to Live Together

Black widow spiders are currently not endangered. They do not face any risk of being wiped off the planet. However, they still face threats from humans, who continue to struggle with fear and misunderstanding about black widows.

It is important to treat any spider bites seriously and to seek medical care as soon as possible. Yet much of the public is unaware that black widow venom rarely causes death in human beings. The biggest threat to human health generally occurs when victims of a black widow spider bite are very young, very old, or in poor health. Luckily, doctors are often able to treat victims with medicines. These medicines fight the unpleasant and dangerous effects of the spider's venom.

Untreated spider bites can become infected and causes serious injuries.

Avoiding Danger and Doing Research

Scientists are working hard to share information with the public that will help them avoid being bitten by black widows in the first place. For example, people should wear long-sleeved shirts and gloves if they plan on working outdoors or in other areas where spiders often nest. In addition, it is best never to tease a spider or try to handle it. Finally, experts say that black widows tend to be less of a problem in locations that are tidy and organized. Keeping clutter out of your home and yard gives spiders less room to hide and build webs.

People still have a great deal to learn about black widows. Researchers hope to find out more about everything from their venom to the incredible strength of their silk. In the meantime, many scientists are eager to prove that the remarkable black widow deserves to be treated with awe and respect instead of anxiety and misunderstanding.

Scientists study black widows carefully to learn more about them.

Words to Know

arachnids (uh-RAK-nidz) — animals such as spiders and scorpions that lack a backbone, breathe air, and have an exoskeleton and four pairs of legs

cells (SELZ) — the smallest units of animals or plants

diameter (dye-AM-uh-tur) — a straight line passing through the center of a circle, connecting opposite sides

endangered (en-DAYN-jurd) — at risk of becoming extinct, usually because of human activity

enzyme (EN-zime) — a protein produced by a plant or animal that causes chemical reactions to occur inside

exoskeleton (ek-so-SKEH-luh-tuhn) — an external supportive covering of an animal

family (FAM-uh-lee) — a group of living things that are related to each other

fossils (FAH-suhlz) — bones, shells, or other traces of animals or plants from long ago, preserved as rock

genus (JEE-nuhs) — a group of related plants or animals that is larger than a species but smaller than a family

glands (GLANDZ) — organs in the body that produce or release natural chemicals

mate (MATE) — to join together to produce babies

metabolism (muh-TAB-uh-liz-uhm) — the rate at which an animal uses energy

molt (MOHLT) — to lose old fur, feathers, or skin so that new ones can grow

nutrients (NOO-tree-uhnts) — substances such as proteins, minerals, or vitamins that are needed by animals and plants to stay strong and healthy

pedipalps (PEH-duh-palps) — small arms near the jaws that help a spider dig, move, and hold on to food

predators (PRED-uh-turz) — animals that live by hunting other animals for food

prey (PRAY) — an animal that's hunted by another animal for food

reproductive (ree-pruh-DUHK-tiv) — having to do with the creation of offspring

species (SPEE-sheez) — one of the groups into which animals and plants of the same genus are divided; members of the same species can mate and have offspring

spinnerets (spin-uh-RETS) — organs for producing threads of silk from the secretion of silk glands

temperate (TEM-pur-it) — describing an area where the temperature is rarely very high or very low

venom (VEN-uhm) — poison produced by some spiders, snakes, insects, and other creatures

Habitat Map

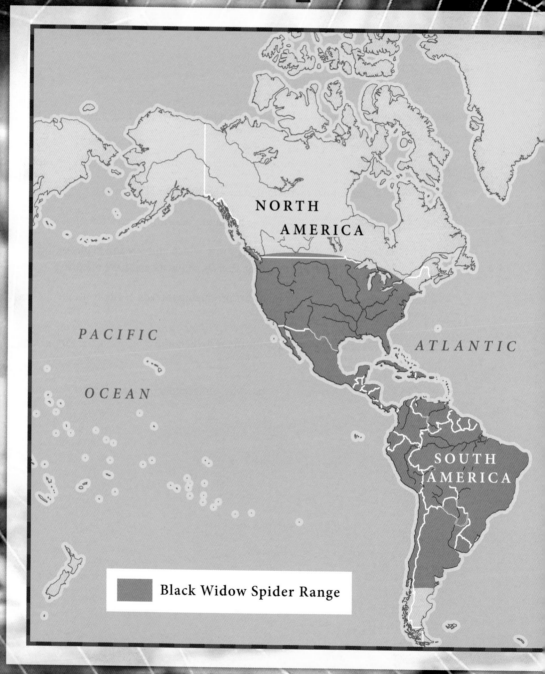

NORTH AMERICA

PACIFIC OCEAN

ATLANTIC

SOUTH AMERICA

Black Widow Spider Range

ARCTIC OCEAN

ASIA

EUROPE

AFRICA

PACIFIC

OCEAN

INDIAN

OCEAN

OCEAN

AUSTRALIA

Find Out More

Books

Kopp, Megan. *Black Widow Spiders*. New York: AV2 by Weigl, 2012.

Markle, Sandra. *Black Widows: Deadly Biters*. Minneapolis: Lerner Publications, 2011.

Owings, Lisa. *The Black Widow Spider*. Minneapolis: Bellwether Media, 2013.

Visit this Scholastic Web site for more information on black widow spiders:
www.factsfornow.scholastic.com
Enter the keywords **Black Widow Spiders**

Index

Page numbers in *italics* indicate a photograph or map.

About the Author

Katie Marsico is the author of more than 100 children's books. She enjoyed learning about black widow spiders, though she hopes to never bump into one in her basement or attic. She dedicates this book to Shelly Messenger, an amazing and much-loved educator.